I0421016

Table of Contents

Introduction

Thank you for downloading/purchasing the book, *Kindle Publishing Unveiled – How to Promote and Sell Your Book*, you are about to discover the secrets of selling books on Amazon.

In this book, you will learn:

- How to promote your book
- What readers are looking for
- Where to promote your book
- What helps your book to sell
- How to use Amazon's promotional tools
- How to choose a good title
- How to increase your sales

Chapter 1: Why it is Important to Promote Your Book

No matter who you are and what product you create, whether it's physical or digital, advertising is one of the major players in increasing profits (in our case, sales). No matter how hard you work to make a high quality product, if you do neglect advertising, your future profits will suffer or even die.

In some cases, product developers have released products that are okay, not even close to the word "quality", but they have invested thousands of dollars in advertising and people started to buy that product just because it's "popular" or because it's a new "trend".

Applying this principle into our case, a book that isn't advertised won't do well.

All the bestselling books on Amazon are bestselling because of 2 factors:

1. The author is very popular and it doesn't need any additional advertising for books on Kindle (even if he invested money in his public image before being popular).
2. As an indie publisher (totally unpopular), you pay for advertising your books among other free methods.

How can you promote your books?

Here's a short comprehensive list:

1. Free websites
2. Paid advertising
3. Promote on Social Media platforms (again – free or paid)
4. Creating a blog to engage readers and to bring traffic to the blog and

then again to the other books (or products)

5. Creating a YouTube channel with dedicated videos for every book

6. Creating a Cross-Promotion series within each book – every book that you have has a chapter at the end that promotes another book of yours. Book A promotes book B, book B promotes book C, book C promotes book D, and so on.

7. Creating an email list from your blog – every time you release a new book, send an email to your followers and encourage them to download and read it by offering them freebies.

Before you start promoting your book, make sure that you do the most important thing of all – Sign up with KDP Select. Without this service, you will only be able to promote your book by dropping the price to $0.99, but you will be limited.

First, I highly recommend to enroll in KDP Select and to give away your book for 5 days every 90 days.

Chapter 2: KDP Promotional Tools

Kindle knows that authors need help to get promoted as fast as possible and Amazon is also directly interested in your sales – the more sales you get, the bigger the profits are for you and Amazon. In other words, you and Amazon depend on each other.

So, Amazon has its own promotional tools, which are:

1. **KDP Select - Free Promotional Days** – You are allowed to promote your book for 5 days every 90 days only if you agree to post exclusively your book on Kindle. What this does is that it offers your book for free for up to 5 days – you can set 24 hours, or 2, 3, 4, or 5 days. It's

your choice on how many days you want to promote it. I tried to promote my books for 3 days or 5 days and the best period to do this is from Sunday to Thursday – it just gets the biggest amount of downloads. When people download your book, your book will automatically rank higher and it will be easier for readers to find your book. The principle is easy: more downloads => higher rank => more sales after the free promotion => more profit.

Step 1		Step 2		Optional	
Your book		**Rights & Pricing**		**KDP Select Benefits**	
✓ Published and available for purchase		✓ In progress			

Run a price promotion for your book on Amazon

Create a new promotion

Sign your book up for one of the following promotional programs

Only one promotional program can be enabled per enrollment period. Please select either Kindle Countdown Deals or Free Book Promotion.

Free Book Promotion >	Create a new Free Book Promotion Deal for this book
	Learn more

Promotions for this book

Promotion Type	Marketplace	Start	End	Duration	Status
Free Book Promotion		December 21, 2014	December 25, 2014	3 day(s)	Complete

2. **KDP Select – Countdown deals –** If you already have a paperback book or you have a very good quality book and you do not want to give it away for free, you can use the countdown deals – you set a base price, and it will rise every day during the 5 days. You are also allowed 5 days every 90 days but you have to choose wisely between free promo days and countdown deal days. There are 5 in total, not 5 for each.

As you can see here, I cannot use countdown deals until the 90 day period ends because I have already chosen to use Free Promo days.

3. **KDP Select – Kindle Unlimited –** You allow your readers to borrow your book and you reach a lot more readers. Don't worry, you get paid as well for borrowed units. This is also available when you enroll in KDP Select program.

The principle is simple. Amazon has a Prime membership currently available for US customers. For a Prime membership, you pay $100/year and you get a lot of benefits such as free shipping for a lot of products, rushed shipping, a lot of features for Amazon Fire TV, free TV programs, as well as an instant access to more than 700,000 books enrolled in KDP Select – Kindle Unlimited. There is a Global Fund each month for Kindle Unlimited and Kindle Online Lending Library (KOLL), in which also I recommend you to enroll in.

The Prime Membership is available only for the US, but there are some countries (Amazon marketplaces where you can have your book borrowed with Kindle Unlimited – customers pay 9.99$/month to borrow books (they have a limited number of borrows for each month).

KU/KOLL has recently become so popular, that now over 40% of the royalties that an author earns are from borrows, so make sure you have already allowed your books to be borrowed. The Global Fund is constantly growing, so more and more customers are likely to join this program.

Borrowed units are marked with a blue line in your dashboard sales like in the picture below:

To summarize this, all you need to know is that KU/KOLL helps you get more sales, more readers, and more money. On average, you get about $1.5/borrow if at least 10% of the borrowed book is read. Usually, most of the borrows are paid, there is very little chance for a person who borrows a book to ignore it or not to read it at all.

4. Amazon Sales Promotion – you get promoted by Amazon after you get a few sales or free downloads (which, in the end, count as sales) by showing your book to other readers – "Customers who bought this, also bought ..."

This helps you reach more readers and get more sales. Amazon does everything for you, all you need to do is wait for the first sales to come.

The same mechanism is for books that have just been viewed – "Customers who viewed this, also viewed…"

5. Bestsellers Rank for Categories and Subcategories – The better you sell your book, the more the book will be promoted by Amazon. You will get into some ranks, at first, in smaller subcategories, and the more sales you get (every day), the better your paid rank and so you will get in the Top #100 of the category the book is put into.

UPDATE 1st July 2015

As a result of the response of authors to the new Kindle Unlimited program, Amazon has decided to change the way they pay authors for loans.

The way Amazon paid authors before 1st July 2015:

If a reader borrows a book and reads at least 10% of the book, a royalty will be paid to the author ((Global Fund + Supplements)/Total Number of Borrows) = $1.35 - $1.5/borrow. This means that whether if you have a book of 10 pages or a book of 400 pages, if someone reads 10% (1 page – or just open the book for the 10 page book, or 40 pages for the 400 page novel) you earn the same royalty, which wasn't fair and encouraged scammers to create short "scamphlets" (scam + pamphlet).

The way Amazon is paying authors after 1st July 2015:

Amazon has decided to redistribute the way they are paying authors. They chose to pay each individual read page. This means that if you have 20 pages, you will be paid for those 20 pages, if you have a 400 page novel, you be paid for 400 pages (if it's fully read).

I just had a look at Amazon and there are over 1,000,000 titles enrolled in KDP Select, from which over 300,000 have less than 30 pages (150,000 have from 1 to 11 pages), so what will happen is this – authors who have books with less than 100-140 pages will earn the same money as before the change (if the book is fully read), authors who have books with less than 100 pages will lose money and authors who have lengthy books with 150

– 500 pages will earn a lot more money than before.

The new system encourages authors to write quality and lengthy books that engage readers. The main authors who will suffer will be scammers, but unfortunately, authors who write Children's Books will also suffer because of the short length. However, images and any graphic content will count as "pages".

The system that counts these pages is the Kindle Edition Normalized Pages (KENP) software.

Chapter 3: The Importance of Keywords

A lot of people do not give too much importance to keywords, but believe it or not, they are responsible for more than 50% of your sales, if they are chosen correctly. A keyword isn't just a word, it's something people are looking for, a small phrase. "How to write a book" for example. You are allowed to choose a maximum of 7 keywords similar to the example I gave you and you have to separate them by a coma.

Now, to choose the best keywords, you have to use Amazon's Search Bar and see what people are looking for. This is a very powerful tool and by using it correctly, you will choose the best keywords that have the biggest number of readers. The more readers you get, the more sales you get, simple as that.

I just typed "how to" and some suggestions appear – the first one has the biggest number of readers, then comes the second, the third, and so on. Depending on what you are writing about, you can choose the best keywords.

But wait, there is another trick to keep in mind. If the keyword is too broad and it has many thousands of results, your book will not be able to outrank those thousands. I mean, it can, but it's almost impossible. On the other hand, if the keyword is too narrow, you will not have too many results, which means not too many people are looking for the keyword you have chosen.

Let's look at some examples, so I can be sure that you got the idea. If I type "how to write a book" I will get 3,436 results so it will be very difficult, nearly impossible, to outrank 3,436 books, so your book will appear on the first page. In other words, the keyword is too broad. Let's go further.

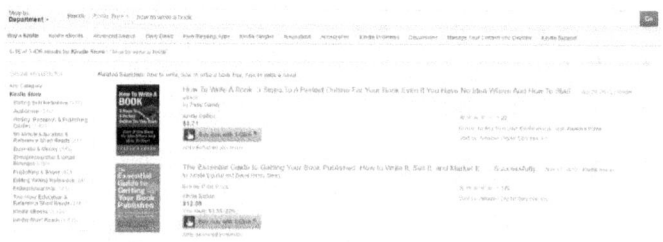

If I type the keyword "how to write the book fast", I will get 101 results, so the keyword is too narrow, there are not enough results and not enough audience.

If I write "how to write and sell a book" I will get 294 results, so it's much better – you will be able to outrank 294 books with a free promo, if used correctly (I will cover how to get more free downloads in the next chapters).

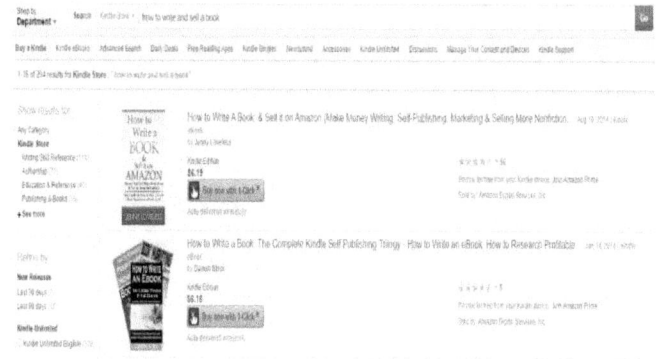

This is just an example. I hope you've got the idea. Try to find the keyword that yielded between 300 and 1,000 results. I think the perfect number is around 500 results, so pick up to 7 keywords with about 500 results (the keywords should be similar or relevant to the title of your book or at least to the content of the book).

Keywords will help you get more free units, more sales, more money, and they will help you rank higher in the searches. And if the book is okay, Amazon will promote it even more. This is essential for the future of your Kindle Books so do not neglect them.

Chapter 4: Reviews

The reviews of a product tell you everything about it. The more reviews, the better it is for your book. The better reviews you get (above 4 / 5 rating), the more sales you get.

People generally judge a product by the cover (or aspect) and the reviews, so this becomes a very important aspect that you may want to take care of by putting the best book you can on Amazon. Every negative review will affect your sales (negatively).

It's difficult to make the first reviews, but by putting your book for free for a number of days, you will get some downloads and some people will take some time to review your book. But in some cases, they don't. The conversion rate is somewhere around 1 review/1,000 free downloads and 1 review/100 purchases. If you get more than that, you are lucky.

When a customer sees a book that has 400 reviews with an overall rating of 4 – oh, my God, I think this book is great and some of them buy it without looking at the sample, page count, or description. Because of this, scammers still survive on Amazon with 5 page books with 50 reviews (fake reviews). They won't be surviving for too long though, and I will tell you why.

On Kindle, you will see books that have over 50 reviews, from which 40 are of 5 stars, and they have 15 pages (full of crappy content with mistakes). In that case, most of the reviews are fake and it's visible from space that the author is trying to artificially raise his ranking and overall rating.

There is nothing wrong with a book that has 5-6 reviews from friends or family just to boost the sales a little bit or to make them start faster, but some authors love to game the system. Unfortunately for them, Kindle came out with the KENP software and they are restricting reviewers severely by flagging their accounts and deleting the reviews one by one.

On Amazon, there are 2 types of reviews: verified purchase reviews, which appears when a customer has downloaded or purchased a book and unverified reviews, which anyone can give an unverified review (most of these reviews come from haters - 1 star reviews or from people who borrow your book and want to write a review).

Negative Reviews

If you release a product or you write a book and you get a negative review, don't panic, it's natural - every single author gets negative reviews on Amazon, even if it's the best book in the world. Some of the comments may be true, but in most of the cases, people write a negative review without justifying their review. You will see reviews like "yawn" or "nope" or "neah" without specifying what they didn't like.

Chapter 5: Promoting Your Book on Websites

It's important to promote your book for your free promo days/countdown deal days to maximize your downloads, and then to get more sales. I will focus now on giving you suggestions on how to promote your book for the free promo days.

Here is a list of websites where you can submit your book. Some of them require a fee to subscribe your book, but they guarantee that they will promote your book accordingly.

Some of the websites are free and some of the websites charge you a fee, and they will promote your book in different places.

www.pixelofink.com

www.bargainbookhunter.com

www.thatbookplace.com

www.ebookshabit.com

www.freebookshub.com

www.ebooklister.com

www.ebooksfreedaily.com

www.frugalfreebies.com

www.onehundredfreebooks.com

www.snicklist.com

www.daily-free-ebooks.com

www.addictedtoebooks.com

Now here's a list with the best paid websites that I've used so far and which I highly recommend you to use for your future books:

For free promotion ($0.00)

- Bookbub
- ENT (ereadernewstoday)
- Freebooksy
- BKnights (Fiverr)
- DigitalBookToday
- BooksButterfly
- BookSends
- BookGorilla
- eBookshabit
- BookTweeters

From this list, I could say that BookBub is by far the best service for promoting a book - you can get 4,000 to 50,000 downloads during the free promotion, but prices are a little high - from $60 to $400 for a book depending on the genre and category. BookBub has its own requirements - you need to have a minimum number of pages, reviews, you need a premium cover and content that has been edited professionally.

Freebooksy is $50 - $100 depending on the genre and it promises somewhere between 1,000 and 7,000 (big numbers come from fiction books).

DigitalBookToday is very good and affordable - for $15 - $50 you can get outstanding results. They have a dedicated category for books that have been recently released.

eBookshabit - They send an email with your book to their subscribers (over 300,000) for $10 and you can get 200 – 1,000 downloads.

ENT - For $25, you can exceed 1,000 downloads easily, but unfortunately, you have to wait a while until you get approved and you have to wait until they schedule you. A slow, but good service.

BooksButterfly guarantees you a minimum number of downloads (NO BOTS). I used their service and they exposing the book to different websites and blogs. If you pay more, will expose your book to websites with higher traffic numbers. You can pay from $50 to $300.

BKnights is a gig from Fiverr who will provide you 100 to 800 downloads for only $5 - the best service for that price. I always use it.

Websites for promoting books at $0.99:

- BargainBooksy
- BuckBooks
- BookSends
- BooksButterfly

About BuckBooks

If there is a service that I can highly recommend to boost your rank, sales, and make some money during the promotion, then try BuckBooks. It's free for authors, but you need a high quality book with at least 40 pages or 10,000 words to get accepted. The cover needs to be clean and you should also have some good reviews for the book (not mandatory).

My results with BuckBooks for one of my books:

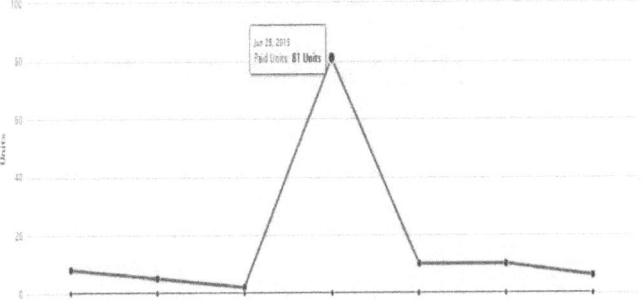

I got those purchases at $0.99 in one day - they don't guarantee you anything, but they told me that I should be expecting between 50 and 200 purchases.

In case you don't have time or you just want to sit more comfortable, you can go to www.Fiverr.com and you can also pay from 5$ to 40$ a gig to promote your book on websites.

Chapter 6: Promoting Your Book on Facebook

Facebook is one of the largest social media websites on which people spend their time every day. Everyone does it, even me and even you, so let's use this powerful tool.

There are a lot of ways to promote your book on Facebook:

1. Creating a Fan Page for your book, or for you, as an author – Put the Fan Page link at the end of every book, people will start following you, so you will get more sales for your upcoming books. You can then promote your Fan Page on other websites as well.
2. Facebook Promote – Pay Facebook to advertise your book/your fan

page – It will help you get more traffic.

3. Use hashtags – Try to post your book on Facebook and use hashtags. Here is a small list of hashtags you may use: #freekindle, #freeebook, #kindle, #KDP, #freebook, #amazon, #goodreads, #freereads, #freestuff, etc. Try to use other ones of your own. Your book will get posted on those hashtags and people will see it.

4. Join Kindle Readers Groups – When you have a book to share or to promote, post it there and tell everyone that you will have a book that will be free. This helps a lot to boost your downloads for the book you want to promote.

Again, if you want your book to be promoted without any effort, go on Fiverr and order a promotion on Facebook (it's based on number 4 – they will promote your book to Kindle Readers secret groups of over 100,000 people or so)

Chapter 7: Promote Your Book on Twitter and Other Social Media Networks

Twitter is also a large social media site you can use to promote your book. Here is a list of where you can go and submit your free book to get additional downloads:

@kindlefreebooks

@kindle_free

@freeebooksdaily

@free2kindle

@pixelofink

@digitalinktoday

@kindlestuff

@kindlenews

@ebook

@free

@freeebookdeal

@freebookdude

@FreeKindleStuff

@IndieKindle

@KindleFreeBook

@KindleBookKing
@KindleUpdates

@Kindle_promo

@Kindledaily

There are a lot of social media networks where you can promote your book, just set up new accounts on Instagram, Pinterest, LinkedIn, Vimeo, etc. There are tons of places where people socialize every day.

Chapter 8: Set Up an Author Central Account

Setting an account on Author Central will help you get access to a lot more readers, people will be able to follow you (subscribe) and they will be notified when you have something new.

People will get the chance to know you better, to read your biography, which will give you better credibility and your sales will increase.

There also statistics there, the rank of the author on Amazon, so you have some other advantages there.

To set up your Author Central Account, go to www.authorcentral.amazon.com

Chapter 9: Pen Names

It's important to have different pen names for different niches that you write about because people get confused when they see one name for different niches. How would it look if I were write under the same pen name, or even my real name, in subjects like mathematics, cookbooks, engineering, diseases, food recipes, automotive, erotic novels, and children's books, all under the same name? Won't you get annoyed? Choose a pen name for one category like health, fitness and dieting, another pen name for business and money, and so on.

By choosing a pen name and posting books on a similar niche, you will become a "local expert" and people who like one of your books will click on your name, will read your biography, and will look at what other books you have for sale.

Chapter 10: Use Box Sets (Bundles)

If you have already posted 2 books that bind well together, or if you have a series of books, combine them 2 in 1. It's very profitable for you and it's also better for readers, they will pay less (that's the point of bundles).

This is just an example, you can use 3in1, 4in1, 5in1, 100in1, however many you like. I usually like to use 2in1 or 3in1. It's enough, I think.

If you have 2 books, and each has 30-50 pages and costs $2.99, instead of selling them at $5.98 separately, you can lower the price to $3.99 or $4.50 for both books.

If you have the books, you only have to make a different cover in which both books are included.

Chapter 11: Title and Subtitle

The title of your book and the subtitle are as important as the keywords. So, how do you make a good title?

1. First of all, describe the BENEFITS that the readers get from your book in the title. You should have at least 1 benefit in your titles, 2 are recommended. The more, the better.
2. The title should be long and descriptive.
3. It has to contain keywords in it, like the ones I showed you above – something like "how to". Use Amazon's search bar to figure out a nice title.
4. Even if the subtitle is optional, make descriptive subtitles and also

try to include a benefit or a keyword.

5. Include your book in a series of books, you will reach more readers as well.

Example of a good title – *Kindle Publishing Unveiled – How to Write, Promote, Market, and Sell Your Book – The Easiest and Fastest Way to Profit on Kindle*

As you can see, I have benefits – obtain profit on kindle fast and easy and I also have keywords – how to write, how to sell, how to market, how to promote your book.

An example of a bad title – *How to Write a Book*. This title does not describe anything, it's foggy, it's not precise, it doesn't show any benefits and it has only one keyword. It's a bad title, is hard to find, and it's not eye catching at all.

Conclusion

Thank you again for downloading this book! I hope you have received the value I have put into this book and I also hope that it will help you in the future.

As I said above, reviews are very important for me to improve my books and to attract more readers, so, dear reader, kindly write an honest review about this book. It will be very appreciated.

Thank you

Kindest Regards